the Golden Thread

Based on a true story of death, grief and healing

written by Brenda Hartman, MSW

illustrated by Zoya Kruse-Wu

The Golden Thread
written by Brenda Hartman, MSW
illustrated by Zoya Kruse-Wu

© 2014 by Brenda Hartman.

First Printing © 2014

All rights reserved. No part of this book may be reproduced in any form whatsoever, by photograph or xerography or by any other means, by broadcast or transmission, by translation into any kind of language, nor by recording electronically or otherwise, without permission in writing from the author, except by a reviewer, who may quote brief passages in critical articles or reviews.

This book does not attempt to diagnose or treat cancer or any other illness. The Golden Thread is based on a true story. Names and certain details have been changed to protect individual privacy.

Print ISBN: 978-0-9882103-2-5
eBook ISBN: 978-0-9882103-3-2

Editing by Karen Carpenter
Illustrations by Zoya Kruse-Wu, www.ZoyaWu.com
Cover design by Suzanne Fyhrie Parrott
Formatted and published by First Steps Publishing

Printed in the United States of America

Please provide feedback

ABOUT THE BOOK

The Golden Thread was written to help children with their grief when a loved one dies.

As a therapist specializing in death and grief, I have worked with many children and their families. I have found it common for children experiencing the death of a loved one to return to the death experience and re-examine it in the light of a new developmental stage and accompanying expanded understanding of the world. At these times, as a loving and trusted person in the child's life, you may be asked questions about the death, including questions you answered previously and thought the child understood. Rereading this book at those times will help the child develop an ever-increasing understanding of the process of death, grief and healing.

Children are often confused by their own and others' feelings as the emotions come and go, especially in the time of grief. This story provides a guide for the healing journey of grief for children of all ages.

The Golden Thread will help children identify the feelings and experiences related to their grief. The story provides an honest, open approach to death. It allows children to begin their developmental understanding of the process of life and death.

The concepts of death and dying are complex and can even be difficult for adults to comprehend. Your children will discuss and explore these concepts directly and indirectly for the rest of their life. This book is intended to be read and reread many times.

May this book be helpful to all the children and adults.

~ Brenda

In The Golden Thread *Brenda Hartman succeeds in weaving together the magical thinking so easily accessed in childhood with the concrete physical reality of grief. This beautifully illustrated book gives name and shape to the undefinable longing that accompanies the death of a loved one.*

~ Anna Leininger, MS,
Certified Genetic Counselor

Both children and adults can mend their broken hearts through this universal story of loss, and cherishing objects that remind us of our loved ones. Poignant and powerful with stunning visuals, The Golden Thread *reminds us we are all connected and we can heal our wounds. Wish I'd had this years ago when I worked in pediatric oncology!*

~ Jeanette Truchsess, R.N., Ph.D.,
Licensed Psychologist, Private Practice

Brenda Hartman, LICSW's beautiful and heartfelt book about death, loss and coping for school age children after the loss of a parent provides solace and light during dark times.

~ Harriet Kohen, LICSW, CPT.
Past President of the Minnesota Society of Clinical Social Work

Tenderly explains the bewildering and painful experience of losing a parent. Beautifully portrays the comfort one boy finds as he learns the gift of love never dies.

~ Meredith Severson, MS, LPC, Psychotherapist

This warm and beautifully illustrated book provides an engaging story while weaving in practical information and creative ideas for children and their parents whom are living with cancer.

~ Janice Haines, Angel Foundation's Facing Cancer Together
co-Director, licensed teacher, two time cancer survivor

*This book is dedicated
to children of all ages who have
experienced the death of a parent. ~ Brenda*

~~

*To my mom, dad, little brother.
Thank you for being in my life! ~ Zoya*

CONTENTS

About the Book ~ 3

The Golden Thread ~ 8

Parent's Guide ~ 48

Acknowledgements ~ 51

Brenda Hartman, Author ~ 53

Zoya Kruse-Wu, Illustrator ~ 53

David's heart was broken. His mother had died. When she died his heart cracked apart.

David was eight and couldn't understand why his mom died. He knew the story of what happened, but his heart was still cracked wide open.

Several years ago, David's mom was diagnosed with cancer. At first, it didn't change many things, just that she lost her hair. She still volunteered at school, and they continued their family hikes.

Then it all changed. David's mom couldn't get out of bed. Her friend Bea came to the house and met with the whole family. They talked about death. It was serious, no one laughed. Instead, they cried.

David wasn't sure what everyone was talking about. David wanted to talk about a summer vacation. But David's dad said they weren't planning any vacations. Bea said that as death approaches, and they are all in "the vigil state," no one plans vacations, everyone stays home.

David waited.

One day, Bea came to their house and told David's mom that she needed to leave the country. Bea was going to adopt a baby.

David heard Bea say to his mom, "You can find me anywhere, soul to soul, when you need me." David wasn't sure what that meant, but he knew Bea said good-bye to his mom in a way that was different from all the other times.

Many people came to the house to say good-bye to David's mom.

Then one night David's mom died. David, his brother, and his dad were all there. It was quiet and peaceful. She stopped breathing and was still. They all cried and held her.

David and his dad didn't know until later that before his mom died she found Bea, soul to soul, in a different country. His mom went to Bea and Bea had a "vivid dream."

In Bea's dream, David's mom came to Bea in a beautiful blue dress and was holding many lit candles in her arms.

Bea and David's mom flew to all the people that loved David's mom. His mom handed a candle to each one. All of them took the candle and held it in front of their hearts.

David's mom then gave one to his brother, one to David and one to their dad. When David's mom had only one candle left, she and Bea flew toward heaven.

They stopped where they would separate. From there, David's mom would enter heaven and Bea would return to the earth. David's mom handed the last candle to Bea. David's mom then turned to the many loved ones that were waiting to greet her and she left the physical world.

David's dad and Bea talked on the phone when Bea returned home. Before David's dad could say anything, Bea gave him a date and time.

David's dad asked her how she knew when David's mom had died. Bea told him about the "vivid dream." The dress and hat she described were the ones David's mom had chosen to be buried in.

Several weeks after David's mom died, David, his brother and dad went hiking to the place they had always gone before with their mom. They hiked to the river. When they got to the place where David and his mom always jumped across the stream, David jumped across.

He looked at his brother and dad on the other side and said, "See you," and off David ran.

David ran to the point where he and his mom would look across the stream toward David's brother and dad on the other side of the bank, where the stream joined the river.

When David arrived at the point, he looked down and found a big, beautiful feather, where his mom usually stood. David picked up the feather. Waving the feather, he yelled to his dad and brother "Mom is here!" David felt the pain in his broken heart, but he also felt some joy at the same time.

Weeks later, David was confused about his feelings. In his bedroom, he would look at the feather he found. He remembered the excitement and closeness he felt to his mom when he found it. And he still felt that his heart was broken and hurt most of the time. He asked his dad if he could talk with Bea. He had questions he wanted to ask her.

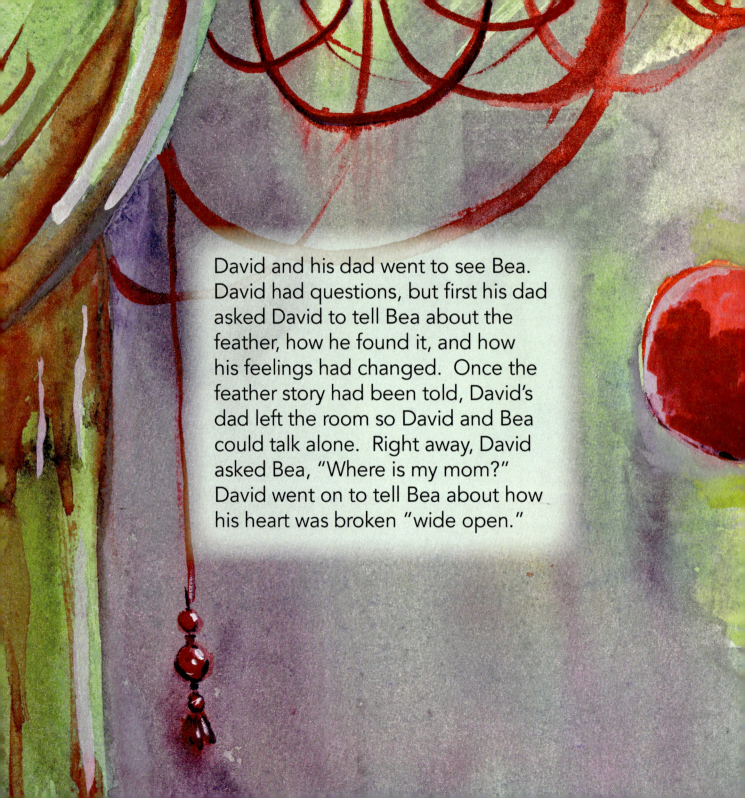

David and his dad went to see Bea. David had questions, but first his dad asked David to tell Bea about the feather, how he found it, and how his feelings had changed. Once the feather story had been told, David's dad left the room so David and Bea could talk alone. Right away, David asked Bea, "Where is my mom?" David went on to tell Bea about how his heart was broken "wide open."

Bea gave David a clipboard with blank paper on it. A cup with markers sat between them on the table. Bea asked David how his heart was made. David knew that one half was from his mom and one half was from his dad. On his paper, David drew half a heart in pink for his mom and half a heart in blue for his dad.

Bea then asked David who else loved him and held his heart. David knew this, too - his brother. David drew a green heart for his brother around the pink and blue heart. Then Bea asked if there was anyone else. David quickly said "my grandfather," drawing a purple heart outside the green heart.

Bea asked David where his heart was broken. David drew a crack through the center of his heart, one side in pink and one side in blue, creating a "wide open" split down the center of his heart.

Bea knew David didn't know about her "vivid dream" about his mother. Bea told David his mom had come to her in a dream before she died and gave candles to all the people she loved, including him. She described how everyone held the candles at their hearts. Looking at David's drawing, Bea pointed to the pink line that created the outside half of his heart. Bea explained how that was when his mom was in her physical body. When she died, David's heart cracked wide open to receive her love into his heart.

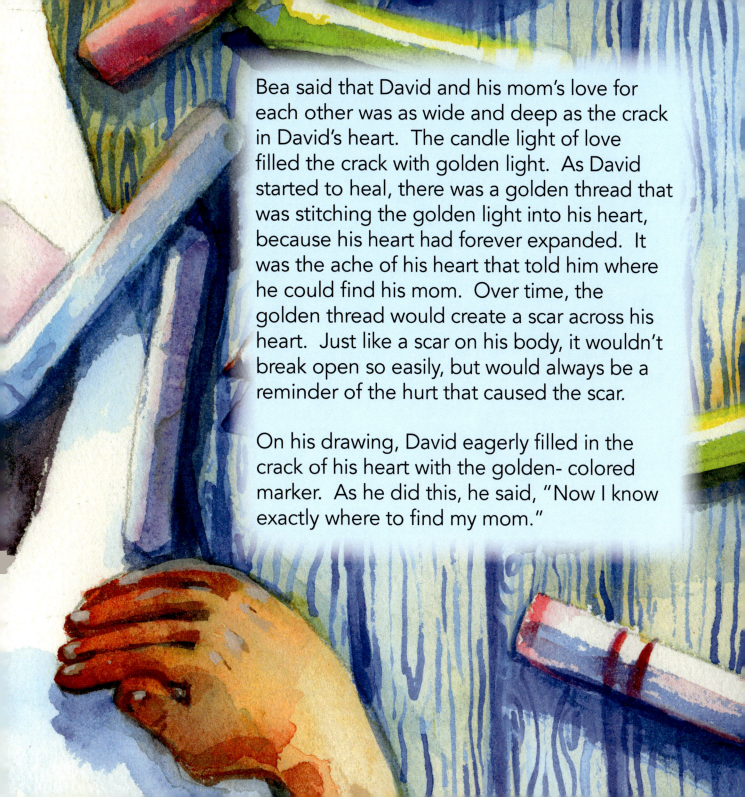

Bea said that David and his mom's love for each other was as wide and deep as the crack in David's heart. The candle light of love filled the crack with golden light. As David started to heal, there was a golden thread that was stitching the golden light into his heart, because his heart had forever expanded. It was the ache of his heart that told him where he could find his mom. Over time, the golden thread would create a scar across his heart. Just like a scar on his body, it wouldn't break open so easily, but would always be a reminder of the hurt that caused the scar.

On his drawing, David eagerly filled in the crack of his heart with the golden- colored marker. As he did this, he said, "Now I know exactly where to find my mom."

David brought his dad back into the room and explained the drawing to him. David explained each color and what they represented, ending with the golden light and the thread that is creating a scar on his heart. He told his dad that his heart had to crack open to receive the love from his mom so he could find her when she was no longer in her body. David's dad was happy that David now knew how to find his mom, and suggested that they frame David's picture to put up in his bedroom.

David left carrying his picture that helped him understand his feelings about his mom dying. When David felt that painful crack in his heart, he now knew he was feeling his mom, missing her physically but connecting to her love.

Parent Guide for *The Golden Thread*

A Guide for Parents and other Adults Reading this Book to Children

It may be helpful for you to read this book by yourself prior to reading it with the child who has experienced a loss. This will enable you to become acquainted with the book's content and know when a child's question will be addressed in the upcoming pages.

Feel free to adapt the book to your individual circumstances. This personalization can be achieved by:

- Leaving out pages
- Changing genders of the book's characters
- Changing the nature of relationships, e.g., death of a grandfather or sibling, or
- Changing the cause of death, e.g., accident, stroke, or old age.

If your child can read, you can point out differences and similarities, e.g., "In the book the little boy's mom died, but your grandmother died." Hopefully, this will create a conversation between the two of you about the experiences, memories, feelings and questions of the child. Additionally, it will help the child understand that every experience with grief and loss is different, and affirm that there is no feeling or experience that is right or wrong.

Some death experiences may "feel" easier, e.g., a grandparent dying of old age as opposed to a younger person dying from an accident. Yet the feelings of sadness, loss and grief are similar throughout the varying experiences of death.

It will help to be mindful of the developmental stage and comprehension level of the child with whom you are reading the book. Preschoolers will have a limited understanding of death. A common phrase they may use when discussing or thinking about death is "the body doesn't work anymore," much like a toy that is broken or a bug that died. This does not indicate a lack of empathy; it is simply a concept that is bigger than the child's understanding.

Children in grade school generally have a more concrete understanding of death. They might ask questions that seem gruesome, e.g., "how long will it take for the worms to eat the body?" This age group is also likely to want to touch the body. They recognize that the body doesn't look or seem exactly right and they want to touch it, which is a way of understanding the process of death. This age group will often run around having fun with their friends at the visitation. They do not grasp the finality of death, much like David in this book. This age group may also feel bad after having fun when they remember that the person died. Most children in this age group do not have multiple mixed feelings at the same time, so being sad with grief and laughing about a funny situation do not occur simultaneously.

Pre-teens and teens understand time in a manner that is much closer to that of adults. Reading this book with them may provoke a conversation about their feelings and experiences without them having to ask any questions. Teens in particular are developmentally working on become self reliant and independent of their parents. This may make it more difficult for them to ask questions directly.

When children ask questions, a good guideline is to give them the simplest explanation that is realistic and honest. Doing so does not imply that information requiring an adult level of comprehension is provided. Rather, it means presenting accurate information which children can understand at their age, and which will establish a foundation for their ever-increasing understanding of death, grief and loss.

Short, simple answers allow children to formulate their next questions over the following days, week, months and years. It is essential to provide an "open door" through which children can ask questions of an adult they can trust to give them "real" and honest answers.

When you do not know the answer to a question, it is helpful and appropriate to say, "I don't know." This will help the children understand they don't need to know all the answers, either. You and the child may want to brainstorm your "best guesses" knowing that there are no definitive, correct answers.

It is important to use the words "death," "died," and "dead." Using phrases such as "went to sleep," "eternal sleep," or "lost to us," can create fear and a lack of understanding. Many children become afraid of going to sleep or worry that their parents will get "lost" and not come back.

Children may think they caused the person to die because of something they said or thought. Telling children that no one can make someone die through thoughts and words will ease unnecessary fears and provide comfort.

As in David's story, drawing out what happened from the child's perspective can also be very healing.

When you do not know what to say, children may be asked about their thoughts, as the answers will provide insight that will help you comprehend what it is they are thinking and/or attempting to understand.

It is normal for children to be sad and have a decreased interest in everyday activities following the death of a loved one. It is beneficial to encourage them to have fun, laugh, and play with their friends, while assuring them that doing so does not mean they did not love the person who died.

You may wonder if your child is grieving "normally." A general guideline is to be aware of significant behavior changes that last two weeks or longer. Such a behavior change might include a child who did well in school previously, but is no longer interested in school and is doing poorly. Areas to assess for dramatic change include eating, sleeping, school engagement, time with friends, family involvement and extra activities.

After the funeral, continuing with the routine of daily life (going to school, sports, lessons, chores, etc.) provides a consistency of safety and comfort for children. This allows them to learn how life continues after a loved one dies, and teaches them that they can find comfort in the familiar. They are incorporating the loss into their developmental level of understanding.

It is important to actively remember the person who died. The first year following the death is often referred to as the "year of anniversaries," because there are so many dates that trigger memories of the last time the loved one was alive for that event, e.g., birthdays and holidays. Creating rituals to allow the child and others to talk about and honor the person who died promotes healing for all. These experiences help guide the child through the process of grief and help them understand that they will always remember the loved one, especially on special days.

While it is difficult to see your child hurting and grieving, recognition of these emotions provides an opportunity for you to assist your child. Death and grief are a part of life, and how you help your child understand and heal through the grieving journey will establish a healthy foundation for a lifetime.

~ Brenda

Acknowledgements

I would like to thank many individuals for their support and participation in the production of this book.

The first step in "David's" story becoming a book was presenting the true story of "David's" mother "Barbara," in *Tell 'em Charlie Sent 'Ya* to a group of colleagues.

When I finished, colleagues **Elizabeth Nager** and **Kathie Bailey** asked what happened to the children. I then shared with them my work with "David" after his mother died, and the story of the "golden thread" that we created. Immediately, through their tears, they both exclaimed that I needed to share "David's" story. Thus, the first step was taken which has ultimately resulted in this book. I am forever thankful to Elizabeth and Kathie for their enthusiasm and the clarity of their vision, which has culminated in the publication of *The Golden Thread*.

It has been a privilege to work with **Zoya Kruse-Wu**, a gifted illustrator. From her first sketch, she was able to capture the depth and power of this story. With each new illustration she showed me, she brought me to tears, as I remembered and felt the experience of being with "David" in each part of the story she illustrated.

My editor **Karen Carpenter** has been a remarkable guide throughout each step. Karen understood the tenderness of the interactions with "David" and helped me articulate this with gentleness.

My publisher **Suzanne Fyhrie Parrott** has been a calming presence. She has provided guidance for each step along the way, helping me create a book that reflects this touching and amazing story.

I have greatly appreciated and leaned on the unwavering support of my sister **Barb**, my daughter **Maria**, and my son **Rob**. Without these three people, this book would never have been written.

I want to thank all of the cancer patients, children and families that I have had the honor and privilege to work with over many years. They have been a source of profound learning for me personally, and for the others with whom I have shared their healing stories.

Most importantly, I want to thank "Barbara," "David's" mom, for trusting me as she approached the end of her physical life and trusting me to work with her family. Their beauty together in healing through "Barbara's" death and the grief thereafter is inspiring and provides hope for us all. May healing come to all who read this book.

~ Brenda

Brenda Hartman, Author

The Golden Thread is Ms. Hartman's second book. Her first book, *Tell 'em Charlie Sent 'Ya,* 2012, is a book of nine stories of healing and death.

Ms. Hartman is a developmental psychotherapist who has worked with children and their families for over 20 years. Ms. Hartman has a specialization in oncology, which brought her to working with "David" and his family ("David's" mother's story "Barbara" is in *Tell 'em Charlie Sent 'Ya,* 2012).

Ms. Hartman has developed and presented programs to over 3000 cancer patients and their families. From her personal experience with stage four ovarian cancer, she has focused her career on helping individuals and families face all aspects of the cancer experience. Ms. Hartman believes it is an honor to walk next to cancer patients and their families, be trusted with their emotional experiences and guide their healing.

The Golden Thread is a true story that Ms. Hartman has shared with many children of all ages, and they have found it to have a healing impact.

You can read more from Brenda Hartman on her website www.HealingThroughLife.com

Zoya Kruse-Wu, Illustrator

Zoya Kruse-Wu is a graduate of MCAD and lives in the Minneapolis area. She has been drawing since she was old enough to hold a pencil. Art is the focus of her life, and *The Golden Thread* is her first professional publication.

See more of Ms, Kruse-Wu's work at www.ZoyaWu.com

Made in the USA
San Bernardino, CA
13 July 2016